NIGERIA

LORNA ROBSON

Evans

TITLES IN THE COUNTRIES OF THE WORLD SERIES:
ARGENTINA • AUSTRALIA • BRAZIL • CANADA • CHINA
EGYPT • FRANCE • GERMANY • INDIA • ITALY • JAPAN
KENYA • MEXICO • NIGERIA • POLAND • UNITED KINGDOM
USA • VIETNAM

Published by Evans Brothers Limited
2A Portman Mansions
Chiltern Street
London W1U 6NR

First published 2005
© copyright Evans Brothers 2005

British Library Cataloguing in Publication Data
Robson, Lorna
Nigeria. – (Countries of the world)
1.Nigeria – Juvenile literature
I.Title
966.9'054

ISBN 0 237 52756 1

Editor: Susie Brooks
Designer: Mayer Media Ltd
Map artwork by Peter Bull
Charts and graph artwork by
Encompass Graphics Ltd

Produced for Evans Brothers Limited by
Monkey Puzzle Media Limited
Gissing's Farm, Fressingfield
Suffolk IP21 5SH, UK

Picture acknowledgements
All photographs were taken by Lorena Ros/
Easi-Images and Roy Maconachie/Easi-Images apart
from the following, which were kindly supplied by:
Link Picture Library/Eric Miller/iAfrika Photos 19, 29
top, 35; Reuters/STR 29 bottom.

Endpapers (front): The streets of Lagos bustle
with people and cars at all hours of the day.
Title page: Markets, such as this one in Benin
City, serve as important arenas for business
and trade.
Imprint and Contents pages: In Nigeria's
delta region, giant oil tankers can be found
alongside traditional fishing boats.
Endpapers (back): One of the old slave ports
near Badagri, from where thousands of slaves
were shipped to plantations in the Caribbean
and America beginning in the sixteenth century.

INTRODUCING NIGERIA 8

LANDSCAPE AND CLIMATE 10

NATURAL RESOURCES 18

ECONOMY 24

ECOLOGY AND ENVIRONMENT 32

POPULATION AND SETTLEMENT 38

LIVING IN NIGERIA 46

DEVELOPMENT AND CHANGE 54

GLOSSARY 58

FURTHER INFORMATION 59

INDEX 60

The Nigerian flag consists of two vertical bands of green, representing agriculture, and one band of white, signifying unity and peace.

Lagos is the most populous city in Nigeria and the African continent.

M odern Nigeria is 'big' in many different ways. It is one of the largest countries in West Africa. It has the greatest population of any African country – one in seven Africans is a Nigerian. It is the main producer of oil in Africa, and is an important contributor to the continent as a whole.

A COUNTRY OF CONTRASTS

Nigeria is a country of extremes and contrasts. Many people are desperately poor, but a few – mainly city dwellers – are extremely rich. The country has an array of beautiful landscapes, as well as huge cities that are as chaotic, polluted and crowded as any in the world.

Nigeria has numerous ethnic and religious groups who speak many different languages. Before European conquest in the nineteenth century, the country was home to an estimated 250 ethnic groups who traded and lived among each other for centuries, but were each governed separately. Since independence in 1960, Nigeria has been a federal republic, which is now divided into 36 states and the Federal Capital Territory of Abuja.

ONE LAND, MANY HISTORIES

Nearly all the ethnic groups of Africa are represented in Nigeria, so the country's history is really a patchwork of these different peoples' pasts. Some of the earliest known settlers were the Nok people of the Jos Plateau in central Nigeria. They established an advanced civilisation around 500 BC, and their tradition for arts and crafts continues today.

From around AD 500, the Hausa and Fulani peoples of northern Nigeria developed strong trading links with North Africa across the Sahara Desert. The Islamic religion was soon introduced along these routes. At the same time, the south-west was dominated by the Yoruba empires, while in the east the Kingdom of Benin developed (not to be confused with today's Benin Republic), and in the south-east the Igbos established their diverse culture.

EUROPEAN IMPACT

The Yoruba kingdoms were the first to make contact with early Portuguese spice traders in the fifteenth century. Then Britain became involved, with trade in other commodities such as palm oil, peanuts, and even slaves. The north remained largely unaffected by contact with the Europeans until the nineteenth century.

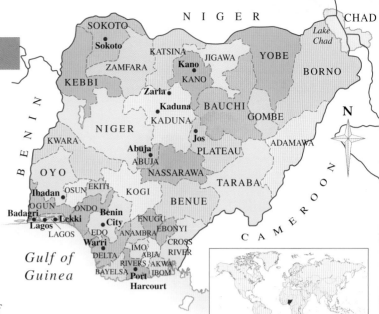

By this time, missionaries had brought Christianity to the south, which began to conflict with the spread of Islam in the north. Religion is still the cause of much unrest in Nigeria today.

In 1861 Nigeria was made a British colony, and by 1914 the country that is now Nigeria was all a British colony. British rule remained until 1960, when Nigeria became a republic as part of a wave of African countries declaring independence.

THE BIAFRA WAR

From the outset of independence there was a power struggle between the different ethnic groups. It seemed that as soon as one government took control, a coup, led by an opposing ethnic group, would take over. In 1967 the Igbos attempted to break away from the rest of Nigeria and declared the Republic of Biafra. This led to one of the most brutal civil wars of the twentieth century. It lasted for three years, by the end of which at least a hundred thousand soldiers were killed and up to two million civilians died of starvation.

MODERN-DAY NIGERIA

In the late 1950s, oil was discovered in commercial quantities in Nigeria. People thought the nation would become rich, but – for a variety of different reasons that will be explained in this book – this did not happen. Nigeria today is struggling to pick up the pieces after decades of military dictatorships, characterised by human rights abuses and repression. The country finally returned to civilian rule and democracy in 1999 under the leadership of President Olusegun Obasanjo.

Nigeria's youthful population is increasing rapidly and is likely to continue to do so in the near future.

KEY DATA

Official Name:	The Federal Republic of Nigeria
Area:	923,770km²
Population:	137,250,000 (2004 estimate)
Official Language:	English
Capital City:	Abuja
Other Main Cities:	Lagos, Kano, Benin City, Ibadan
GDP Per Capita:	US$860*
Currency:	Naira (NGN)
Exchange Rate:	US$1 = 129.51 naira £1 = 243.94 naira

*(2002) Calculated on Purchasing Power Parity basis.
Sources: World Bank; UN

LANDSCAPE AND CLIMATE

Mangrove swamps line the south coast and provide a unique ecosystem for birds and fish.

Nigeria is generally a fairly flat country, but it has a wide range of different landscapes. These include dry semi-deserts, open grasslands and hills, mountainous areas, tropical rainforests and mangrove swamps.

LAND USE

About 40 per cent of Nigeria's land surface is used for intensive crop agriculture. Pasture for grazing animals, such as cattle and goats, takes up another 20 per cent, while just over 6 per cent is forest and woodland. Two major rivers flow through Nigeria – the Niger and the Benue.

ROCKS AND SOILS

The land and soils of much of north and south-west Nigeria are formed from old, igneous, crystalline rocks which are part of the African Shield. This is an ancient layer of very hard rocks that are resistant to erosion, and so the plateaux and hills here are quite high. The rocks

LANDSCAPE FEATURES

Nigeria's remaining tropical rainforests are a rich resource, but they are threatened by human use in some regions.

are rich in minerals, providing Nigeria with some valuable natural resources. The soils tend to be fertile, with high levels of nutrients, though in the north this is not always the case.

In the south-east, and the low-lying north-east and north-west corners of the country – the Chad and Sokoto Basins – the land is made up from younger sedimentary rocks. These form light, sandy soils but they are less fertile and less resistant to erosion than the older rocks described above.

LANDSCAPES OF THE SOUTH

Southern Nigeria borders the Atlantic Ocean. The coastline extends for 800km and consists mainly of low sedimentary plains.

THE NIGER DELTA

The delta of the River Niger juts into the Gulf of Guinea in the eastern Atlantic. It is one of the largest river deltas in the world and is Nigeria's main oil-producing region. The delta covers a huge area and is an intricate network of streams, mangrove swamps, islands, lagoons and sand bars.

THE COASTAL LOWLANDS

To the east and west of the delta are the coastal lowlands – areas of sandy beaches, indented by numerous palm-fringed lagoons and creeks.

These lowlands rarely rise over 30m above sea level. Lagos – the largest city in sub-Saharan Africa – is built on an island created by West Africa's biggest lagoon. Harbours are scattered nearby, but constant dredging is needed because sand levels are high. This is due to the Guinea Current which moves material along the coast.

HILLS, PLAINS AND PLATEAUX

Stretching inland from the coast is an area of low, gently undulating plains and scattered hills, covered in thick tropical rainforest. This extends for about 250km, then continues up into the basins of the Niger and Benue rivers.

LOCATING NIGERIA

Nigeria lies north of the Equator between latitudes 4° North and 14° North and between longitudes 3° East and 15° East. It measures from east to west 1,200km and from north to south 1,050km at its widest points. It is bordered by Benin to the west, Niger to the north, Chad to the north-east and Cameroon to the east. To the south is the Atlantic Ocean.

Nigeria's coastal waters provide local fishermen with an important livelihood, here near Badagri.

INLAND LANDSCAPES

Moving inland from the coastal region, the land rises to escarpments of dipping rock strata. These form the rocky terrain of the central plateaux. To the east are Nigeria's mountains, while in the far north-east and north-west the landscape is low and flat.

THE EASTERN HIGHLANDS

The Eastern Highlands are the only mountains in Nigeria. They lie along the border with Cameroon and are made up of several separate ranges and plateaus. In the Shebeshi Mountains is Nigeria's highest point – Dimlang (2,042m) – sometimes known as Vogel Peak. Also in this area are crater lakes with warm thermal springs, created by ancient volcanoes. Many swift-flowing rivers have their source in these mountains and flow into the River Benue. The area is sparsely populated.

THE CENTRAL AND NORTHERN PLATEAUX

North of the valleys of the Niger and the Benue, and around the centre of the country, lies a fairly flat plateau area. The average height

above sea level is about 700m. Rivers have cut into the plateau, eroding the rock. The vegetation is open grassland – known as savannah – which is occasionally interrupted by outcropping granite hills called inselbergs. This is Nigeria's main agricultural area and it is heavily populated.

The vegetation becomes sparser – fewer trees and shrubs – and the climate drier the further north you go. The land extends through a relatively fertile region, where Nigeria's main grazing is found, to a dry expanse in the extreme north. This is known as the Sahelian zone and is basically an area of semi-desert.

THE CHAD AND SOKOTO BASINS

The north-eastern and north-western tips of Nigeria form the Chad and Sokoto Basins. Here, the land drops to below 300m, forming depressions into which rivers drain. The Sokoto River and its tributaries flow through the Sokoto Basin and deposit large quantities of sediment to create broad flood plains. This area is also highly

Yankari National Park is an important wildlife sanctuary, but it is also known for its hot springs.

Jos has a temperate climate because of its elevation, and is well suited for dairy farming and vegetable production.

The Jos Plateau is a relatively high area of granite and volcanic rocks. It covers an area of about 8,000km^2, rising out of the middle of Nigeria and forming the largest land mass over 1,000m. With its rugged terrain of volcanic plugs jutting out of wide savannah grasslands, some of the scenery on the plateau is spectacular. On the south-west slopes, heavy rainfall feeds small patches of rainforest.

The plateau forms a watershed from which streams flow to Lake Chad in the north and to the rivers Niger and Benue to the south. The higher altitudes and cooler temperatures combine to draw rainfall from passing clouds. Because of its pleasant climate and the fact that it is freer from diseases than the surrounding lowlands, this region has one of the highest population densities in the country. During the colonial era this is where many Europeans liked to live. The rich soils and favourable climate provided an excellent environment for growing European vegetables, such as potatoes, and also for a dairy industry.

The town of Jos (with a population of 510,300) is the major settlement on the plateau, despite the fact that Nigeria's capital Abuja (population 107,069) is also located here. Jos is considered by many to be Nigeria's most attractive city. It grew up around tin mines at the beginning of the twentieth century. Tin is still mined and processed in this area, although the industry has declined in recent years because aluminium is now more widely used.

influenced by wind action and is often covered by drifting sands. Both basins are intensively cultivated with the help of irrigation. Low-lying wetland areas, or *fadamas* (see page 21), are particularly important sites for agriculture. Artesian reservoirs – aquifers of water stored below the ground – are another useful source of water here.

Zuma Rock, a famous granite outcrop, marks the edge of Abuja.

CLIMATE

Nigeria's climate is hot all year round, with distinctive rainy seasons. The country lies entirely within the tropics, yet there are wide climatic variations. The main difference between the north and the south of the county is the much higher rainfall and humidity nearer the coast. In addition, the higher land of the Jos Plateau and the Eastern Highlands tends to be cooler than elsewhere.

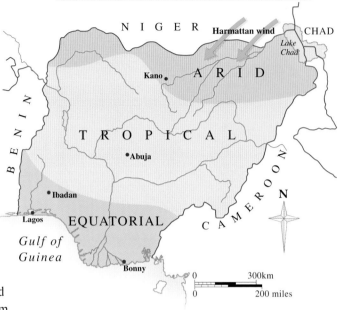

NIGERIA'S SEASONS

In Nigeria it is more common to talk about rainy and dry seasons than summer and winter. Nigerian seasons are controlled by the movement of two air masses – warm, moist air from the Atlantic and hot, dry air from the Sahara Desert. The area where they meet is called the inter-tropical convergence zone. During the summer months of April to September this zone moves slowly northwards, bringing most of the country under the influence of moisture-laden maritime air. This is when Nigeria experiences its rainy season. Then the zone moves south, leaving the north exposed to the hot, dry, Saharan air mass again.

THE VARIABLE NORTH

The rainy season in the north lasts from late May to the end of September. The Hausa people divide the seasons into four main categories – the dry, cool season *(kaka)*, the dry, hot season *(bazara),* the wet, warm season *(damina)* and the dry, warm season *(rani)*.

The beaches and sunshine of the south coast, here on the Lekki Peninsula, are popular for day trips.

Leading up to the rainy season, between March and May, temperatures can reach as high as 45°C. They can fall as low as 6°C at night time during December and January. The average rainfall in the north is 500–750mm. However, for at least five months of the year, there is no rainfall at all and the area sometimes suffers from droughts. Droughts have become more frequent in recent years and experts say the last 100 years have been among the driest for several centuries. Droughts in the 1970s and 1980s severely affected large areas of northern Nigeria; crops failed, cattle died and in some cases, people died too. It is possible that these droughts are part of a much larger change in the world's climate as a whole.

THE EQUATORIAL SOUTH

The climate in the south can be described as equatorial. This means it is generally hot and wet for most of the year. It is strongly affected by the moist air mass that moves northwards from the Atlantic Ocean.

The most rainfall comes between April and July and in September and October, and it can be extremely heavy. Bonny, a town on the south-east coast, has an average rainfall of more than

The equatorial south receives heavy rainfall, especially during September and October.

4,000mm per year. This is five times the annual rainfall of London, UK or Minneapolis, USA. People are advised to keep water channels and drains clear in order to avoid flooding, which is a common problem. Although the temperatures here are, on average, slightly cooler than in the north, the high humidity makes it feel much hotter and more uncomfortable.

CASE STUDY
THE HARMATTAN WIND

The Harmattan is a dry wind that blows in from the Sahara Desert between November and March, bringing tiny particles of sand. These form a hazy cloud or fog that can block out the sun. The sand covers everything – buildings, cars, people – with a fine film of dust. This gets into people's eyes and sometimes causes infections such as conjunctivitis. The Harmattan dust occurs mainly in the north of Nigeria, although it also spreads as far south as the coast. It has even been known to reach the UK. Here it is called 'blood rain' and coats cars with red dust around March.

Dust carried by the Harmattan winds provides farmers near Kano with rich soil nutrients.

TEMPERATURE AND RAINFALL

KEY:
Temperature   Rainfall

RIVER SYSTEMS

The rivers of Nigeria are important assets. They provide sources of energy, transport routes, food and water for both domestic use and irrigation. The two largest rivers – the Niger and the Benue – form a 'Y' shape that effectively divides the country into three. They meet almost at the centre of the country. This is seen as the symbolic meeting point of the country's different ethnic and religious groups and is therefore an important site.

THE NIGER AND ITS TRIBUTARIES

The River Niger is the third-largest river in Africa and the sixth-largest in the world. Of its 4,170km length, only a third lies within Nigeria, but it is still the country's longest and most important river. About two-thirds of Nigeria's land is within its catchment area.

The Niger's source is in the hills of Futa Jalon in Guinea. It enters Nigeria from the west and flows in a south-easterly direction until it is joined by its major tributary, the River Benue, at Lokoja. The Benue is Nigeria's second-most important river. Its source is in the hills of Cameroon and it enters Nigeria from the east.

Other important rivers in Nigeria are the Sokoto, Kyobe, Hadejiia and Kaduna in the north and Ogun, Osun, Owena, Osse, Anambra and Cross River in the south.

HYDROELECTRIC POWER

The Niger and the Benue are important sources of hydroelectric power (HEP). The Kainji Dam, near Jebba, was built on the Niger in 1968 to provide power as well as water to irrigate the surrounding area. Since the building of a series of dams on the River Niger and at Shiroro Gorge on the Kaduna River, 38 per cent of Nigeria's energy needs have been met through hydroelectricity. Power from these plants is distributed to the large towns and cities. However, many villages in Nigeria are still without any electricity at all – they burn wood as their main energy source. What is more, dam-building has had serious consequences for local populations, ousting

The Niger is Nigeria's most important river, and the land around its tributaries is farmed and settled intensively.

The Kainji Dam on the River Niger is Nigeria's largest dam.

farmers from their land, interrupting pastoral routes and causing severe flooding hazards (see case study).

TRANSPORT AND DREDGING

Nigeria's rivers tend to get silted up, which makes them shallow and unnavigable for large boats. In 1998, the Nigerian Government decided to start dredging the Niger and the Benue from central Nigeria to the Niger Delta. The aim was to deepen the rivers and keep the water flowing, making them better equipped to ship goods and people. However, several environmental groups objected, and many river-bank communities were worried how the dredging might affect their jobs and their villages.

Particular concern has been expressed about the impact on the Niger Delta. This area already suffers from oil pollution. There is now concern that the increased flow of the River Niger might speed the rate at which the river banks are eroded and lead to flooding.

Local groups protested against the dredging, particularly in the Niger Delta where they felt the only people who would benefit would be the mining companies. This held things up, but in 2004, after a protracted delay, the Federal Government commenced plans to dredge the River Niger again.

CASE STUDY
FLOODING

The damming of Nigeria's major rivers for irrigation and hydroelectricity has caused incidences of serious flooding in recent years.

In 2003, heavy rains led to dangerously high water levels that threatened to burst the walls of the Shiroro Dam on the Kaduna River. Officials decided to open the gates of the dam to prevent this – but more than 100 villages downstream were flooded in the process. No lives were lost because villagers were given warnings, including radio broadcasts, before the waters were released. However, homes, schools, hospitals and fields of crops were destroyed, or damaged beyond affordable repair. In other cases warnings have not been given and many lives have been lost. In October 2004, flash flooding severely damaged a church building and a home for the elderly in the southern Nigerian state of Akwa Ibom, following particularly heavy rainfall.

Small boats provide an important mode of transport in the south. Many rural roads become impassable during the rains.

This refinery outside Port Harcourt processes crude oil into petroleum for local consumption.

N igeria is rich in natural resources. It is the world's sixth-largest producer of crude oil, has huge reserves of minerals and boasts plenty of fertile land that is suitable for agriculture. Its large population constitutes a skilled workforce and creates a huge market for home-produced products.

Nigeria is potentially Africa's wealthiest country. However, this potential has yet to be realised, and very few Nigerians gain any benefit from their country's assets. Many of Nigeria's natural resources have not been exploited. This is partly because of a lack of investment – either by the government or by foreign investors – and partly because successive governments have failed to plan properly for development.

OIL – THE 'BLACK GOLD'

Crude oil, sometimes known as 'black gold', is by far Nigeria's most important and most exploited resource. In the late 1950s, vast reserves of crude oil were discovered in the Niger Delta region. Nigerian oil, which is known as 'Bonny Light', has a low sulphur content. This makes it particularly attractive to American and European buyers as it produces less-polluting petroleum, which helps them meet the legal requirements for 'clean fuel' and is easier to turn into gasoline.

REFINING OIL

There are four oil refineries in Nigeria. Three are located in the Niger Delta region and one in northern Nigeria at Kaduna. Oil is transported to the north by pipeline. By processing the oil themselves – turning it from crude oil into petroleum – Nigeria can make more profit.

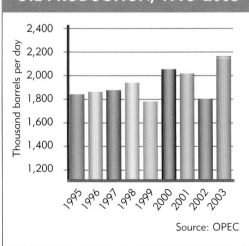

OIL PRODUCTION, 1995–2003

Thousand barrels per day

Source: OPEC

However, the refineries often operate at only 40 per cent of full capacity. They are poorly maintained, under-funded, and from time to time have been the target of sabotage by people who object to what the oil industry is doing to their land. As a result, much of Nigeria's oil is exported and refined abroad.

FUEL SHORTAGES

Nigeria produces 90 million tons of crude oil a year, but as most of this goes to the international market, Nigeria itself sometimes suffers from fuel shortages. It is therefore forced to import about 70 per cent of its fuel from other countries. When Nigerians go to fill up their cars with petrol, they often find that there is none there, or that the prices have rocketed because of the black market. Thousands of illegal fuel salesmen sit along the roadside selling at very high prices. Large amounts of domestic fuel disappear across the borders to Chad, Niger, Benin and Cameroon, where locals have to pay up to four times as much for petrol. This angers many Nigerians who think they should have access to cheap petrol, given that their country produces so much. There have been several strikes as a result.

Surface pollution from oil wellheads near Soku has caused environmental damage.

NATURAL RESOURCES

≋ Major HEP plant
⛏ Oil and gas
🪨 Coal
⬮ Thermal power
Ⓕⓔ Iron ore
Ⓒⓑ Columbite
Ⓢⓝ Tin
Ⓛ Limestone
Ⓡ Rubber
Ⓒⓔ Cement
Ⓣ Textiles
Ⓦ Wood processing
Ⓜ Motor vehicle assembly

ENERGY DEMANDS

With Nigeria's vast and rapidly growing population, huge amounts of energy are required to meet domestic, manufacturing and business needs. In urban areas in particular, the demand for energy is increasing. More and more consumer products, such as washing machines and computers, are being used, even though the majority of Nigerians still can't afford these luxuries. Fuel resources, therefore, are a valuable commodity.

NEW RESERVES

The oil industry is expanding because of the discovery of new offshore oil fields near Akwa Ibom. These deposits are more expensive and difficult to extract, but companies are keen to move away from the Niger Delta where they have experienced protests and demonstrations from local people over the use and pollution of their lands (see case study page 35).

ABOVE: Much of Nigeria's oil and gas is loaded onto tankers and exported for processing into other products such as fuels and chemicals.

BELOW: Tin miners near Jos. Tin mining, once a major industry on the Jos Plateau, has declined in importance since aluminium has replaced many of the uses for tin.

UNEXPLOITED MINERALS

Nigeria possesses an abundance of mineral resources other than oil. Unfortunately, most of them remain unexploited. Any kind of mining requires huge initial capital investment, and Nigeria is unable to afford this. There is some foreign investment, but many countries are still reluctant to invest in Nigeria following its recent political instability.

NATURAL GAS

Natural gas is found in abundance alongside oil in the Niger Delta. In 2001, annual production was about 15.7 billion m^3 and Nigeria has 5 per cent of the world's estimated totals. Anticipating major development of this resource, a large-scale project was started in 1999 to export natural gas from Bonny Island in the Niger Delta. There are also plans to pipe gas north across the Sahara Desert to Algeria and on to Europe.

MINERALS AND MINING

There are sizeable deposits of iron ore in the savannah region in the northern half of the country. This iron ore is generally of a low grade, but it is important for the steel industry. Nevertheless, iron ore still needs to be imported to meet demands within Nigeria. Limestone is another raw material used in the steel industry and is quarried in the valleys of the Niger, Benue and Sokoto rivers.

Lignite (brown coal) and sub-bituminous coal are found and mined in the south-east of Nigeria. There are significant coal reserves, but the government has neglected these in favour of the oil industry. Tin and columbite are mined on the Jos Plateau, although tin mining is declining as world prices are now so low.

There are plans to exploit Nigeria's reserves of bauxite (the natural ore of aluminium) and develop its aluminium industry. Aluminium is important in the manufacture of lightweight products such as food cans. The problem is, as with nearly all of Nigeria's resources, that the capital investment is lacking.

WATER FOR IRRIGATION

Water is vital for irrigating agricultural land, especially in the dry regions of northern Nigeria where droughts are common. The first government irrigation projects began

Irrigation using the traditional pulley and oxen system is still common in many parts of the north.

more than 50 years ago and, by the end of the 1960s, 9,000 hectares of land were under irrigation. There are major large-scale irrigation schemes such as the South Chad Irrigation Project in Borno state and the Kano River Project, funded by the federal government in the 1970s. The money for these came mainly from the revenues from oil. Over-spending on such projects has been largely responsible for the huge debt that Nigeria currently faces (see page 25).

TRADITIONAL METHODS

Many traditional irrigation methods are still used. Sometimes shallow depressions of land are created and flooded during the rainy season to conserve water. This is known as water harvesting. Particularly important for agricultural production and livestock grazing are the naturally occurring *fadamas* – seasonally water-logged areas or stretches of flooded low-lying land. In the north, *shadoof* irrigation has been operating for hundreds of years. This is where a pivoted pole, with a weight at one end and a bucket at the other, is used to raise water from a well or a river. In some parts of the north, people are able to use artesian wells, where water is driven to the surface from underground reserves.

Cattle rearing is important in the north, but it is becoming increasingly difficult for traditional pastoralists to make a living.

FOOD FROM THE LAND

A variety of crops grow well in Nigeria's climate and 33 million hectares of land are under cultivation. Many rural households and farms have chickens to provide eggs, and goats and sheep are kept for their meat. Cattle are reared on the plains of the north, but there is an increasing danger of over-grazing in these areas.

HOME PRODUCE

Most of the crops grown in Nigeria are subsistence crops – produced by farmers for their own family use, with any surplus sold at the market. In the north, grains – such as sorghum and millet – are the staple crops. They are typically intercropped (see page 36)

Many subsistence farmers still use the 'bucket method' to irrigate their crops.

with cowpeas and groundnuts. The wetter climate in the south is more suitable for rice, maize and yams. Cassava and tomatoes are grown throughout Nigeria.

CASE STUDY
A COCOA FARMER

Nigeria is the world's fourth-largest producer of cocoa, with 6 per cent of the total supply, and cocoa is Nigeria's largest source of foreign income after oil. However, cocoa yields have been falling steadily since the 1970s, because farmers have been reluctant to cut down their overaged trees and replace them with more productive new varieties and because the rural infrastructure is poor.

Alowonie Williams is a farmer in his mid-50s. He grows cocoa pods on his plantation near the town of Akure in the state of Ondo. Alowonie is one of 11 million people in West Africa who depend on cocoa production for their livelihood. He has seen his cocoa yields and his income fall since he started farming, and he knows that he needs to replace his old trees. But he says he can't afford to lose more income in the short term while he waits for the new trees to mature and become productive.

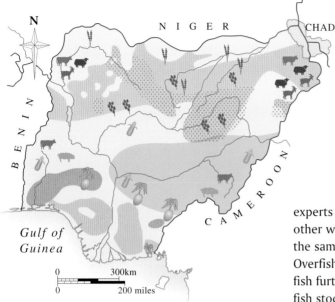

N

NIGER

CHAD

BENIN

CAMEROON

Gulf of
Guinea

0   300km

0   200 miles

Peanuts   Sorghum

Cocoa   Cattle

Rice   Sheep

Oil palm   Goats

Cotton   Pigs

Millet   Yams

Maize   Cassava

CROPS FOR EXPORT

Palm oil became an export crop to Europe
during the nineteenth century and was used to
lubricate machines in the factories and mills of
England. It is now exported for the production
of margarine and ice cream. Cocoa, from which
chocolate is made, is another important
commercial export crop – 60 per cent of
Nigeria's annual cocoa output comes from the
so-called 'cocoa belt' in the Ondo region.

FOOD FROM RIVERS, LAKES AND THE SEA

Fish from Nigeria's rivers, lakes and from the
sea are an important source of food. Lake
Chad and the Kainji Reservoir are particularly
rich in fish. Traditionally, fishing has been
done from dug-out canoes; the main
difference today is that they have outboard
motors. Sea fishing is based in small fishing
villages all along the south coast. Boats set
out to sea in search of bonga and sardinella.
Fishing plays a vital role in supplying a large
number of people in Nigeria with affordable,
high-quality animal protein.

THREATENED STOCKS

Shrimp are fished for commercial purposes in
the Gulf of Guinea – mostly for export. The
catch is estimated at 4,700 tonnes a year, but
experts consider that this is unsustainable. In
other words, if people keep catching shrimp at
the same rate, the stocks will soon run out.
Overfishing by foreign-owned trawlers, which
fish further out to sea, is also rapidly depleting
fish stocks. Furthermore, pollution associated
with the oil industry has seriously affected
marine life in the Niger Delta. These factors
could have disastrous results for the small
coastal communities that depend on fish for
their livelihoods.

The size of fish catches today may be smaller
than in the past due to threatened stocks.

Lagos is an important industrial city and is the 'economic engine' of Nigeria.

Since the 1970s, Nigeria has depended very heavily on the income it gets from oil – too heavily. Oil revenues account for 80 per cent of government earnings and 90 per cent of foreign exchange earnings. This means that the health of the Nigerian economy is very closely linked to world oil prices. If these fall, the country suffers.

HISTORY OF TRADE

Nigeria's economy has been closely linked to international markets in one way or another for several hundred years. Before the Europeans set foot in Nigeria, there was a thriving trade in all types of commercial goods such as cotton cloth, palm oil, earthenware pots and raffia mats. These were sold across the Sahara Desert to North Africa and beyond, and in the south along the Atlantic coast.

THE SLAVE TRADE

The growth of the slave trade, between the beginning of the sixteenth century and the middle of the nineteenth century, had a devastating effect on Nigeria – and Africa as a whole – in both humanitarian and economic terms. It is estimated that Africa lost more than 20 million people to the plantations of the Caribbean and America. Often the strongest and most able men and women were taken and transported across the Atlantic, leaving farms without workers.

BOOSTING THE BRITISH EMPIRE

During the nineteenth century, when Britain increased its power over Nigeria, goods were exported to Britain. Nigeria supplied raw materials such as cotton and palm oil for the British Industrial Revolution.

OIL BOOM

Following the discovery of oil in the late 1950s, the face of the Nigerian economy was completely changed by the 1970s. With the vast revenues and income Nigeria was getting from oil, the country looked set for a very prosperous future. Many people thrived, and

The gates of the former Badagri slave encampment. Slavery had a major impact on the farming economies of Nigeria.

those in a position to take advantage of Nigeria's new status and wealth – mainly politicians and their families – made a lot of money.

The government started to invest in the country's infrastructure – it spent money on education, healthcare, industrial development, and on several vastly expensive schemes such as building dozens of new universities and roads. These schemes increased employment, particularly in the construction industry.

OIL BUST

Confident its wealth would continue to materialise, the government took out loans from international lenders to boost its development projects. Nigeria began to import expensive Western consumer goods, such as cars, and huge sums were spent on urban improvement projects.

But in the early 1980s, oil was plentiful worldwide – in fact there was a glut – and the price fell dramatically. Nigeria had been depending almost entirely on its oil revenues, so the bubble burst. Projects had to be abandoned and the country fell into an economic depression.

Interest rates rose as fast as oil prices had dropped, and Nigeria faced huge difficulties in repaying the loans it had taken out in better days. International lenders and creditors started to call in their loans, imposing strict restrictions on the way in which the

ECONOMIC STRUCTURE (% GDP CONTRIBUTIONS), 2004

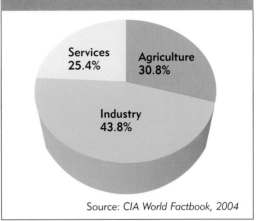

Source: *CIA World Factbook, 2004*

GNI PER CAPITA (US$)

Source: World Bank

government could spend money on social programmes such as education and health. These restrictions were part of what is known as a Structural Adjustment Programme.

MAJOR TRADING PARTNERS (% OF VALUE), 2002

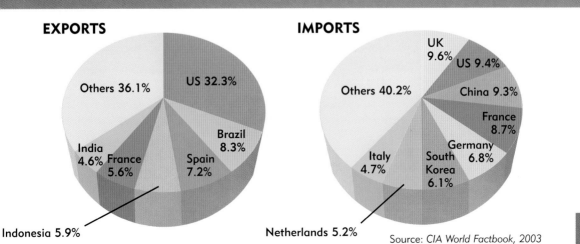

Source: *CIA World Factbook, 2003*

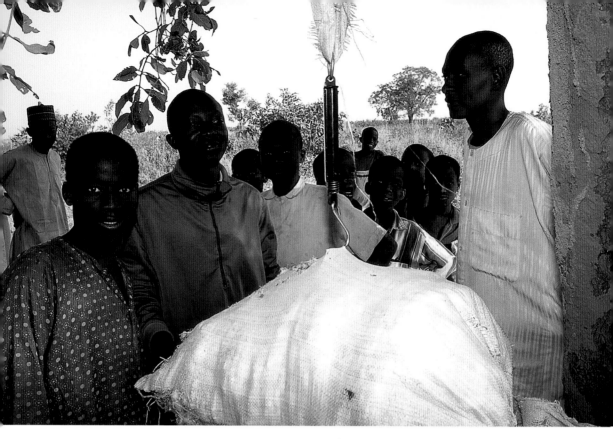

AGRICULTURE

At the time of independence, in 1960, agriculture was still Nigeria's main source of foreign income. The Nigerian government tried to boost the domestic economy by encouraging firms to use local materials instead of relying on imports.

The oil boom had a serious effect on agriculture. In the early 1970s, when the price of crude oil was high, Nigeria could afford to import exciting new consumer goods, including agricultural produce. But these imports undermined locally produced foods and farm products, and many farm workers flocked to the cities. During the 1980s, the government adopted a ban on the import of wheat – the staple of people in towns – in order to encourage self-sufficiency in wheat production. However, many farms were abandoned and many never fully recovered. Today agriculture is still important in terms of producing food crops, and it provides employment for a large majority of the population. But Nigeria, once self-sufficient and a large exporter of food, now has to import food.

Cotton being weighed before transport to market. Cotton is one of several cash crops grown in northern Nigeria.

MANUFACTURING

Nigeria's manufacturing industry is dominated by light consumer goods, such as textiles and drinks. Other products include motor-vehicle parts, pharmaceuticals and foodstuffs. However, industry is highly dependent on the import of expensive raw materials and is therefore not as profitable as it could be. Likewise, Nigeria has to pay high prices for imported machinery, which prohibits development in terms of producing more goods. Manufacturing employs only about 8 per cent of the workforce.

The problems exist because, in the past, a large part of Nigeria's manufacturing industry was owned by foreign companies. The Lebanese in particular have a long tradition of setting up businesses all over West Africa, especially in Nigeria. The country has attempted to change this situation so that more factories are owned and run by Nigerians using local materials.

ABOVE: Billions of dollars have been wasted on 'white elephant' projects in Nigeria, such as the Ajaokuta steel plant.

CASE STUDY
REVITALISING THE STEEL INDUSTRY?

The Ajaokuta steel plant is located in Ajaokuta in Kogi state and occupies an area of 24,000 hectares. It was originally designed in 1979 to produce 1.3 million tonnes of liquid steel per annum. It was begun with Soviet funding and engineers from the USSR were involved in its construction. However, in 1983 the project lost its funding and the plant fell into disrepair.

Following the restoration of democratic rule in 1999, the government – with help from the World Bank – undertook to renovate the plant. The original plant was by then very outdated and the Nigerian government had to spend more than US$5 billion on renovating and reactivating it. At the beginning of 2004, an Indian company was commissioned to continue the rehabilitation and eventual handover of the plant to the Nigerian government. However, by October 2004, the plant had closed down.

This would reduce imports which would save money and bring more work.

Most of Nigeria's manufacturing industry is located in the south around Lagos. Attempts are being made to move production elsewhere, to avoid too much concentration in this already crowded area. The hope is also to base industry more and more on the use of local resources.

DIVERSIFICATION

Nigeria needs to look at how it can develop other industries so that the economy can become more diverse. Foreign investment would help to exploit some of the country's rich resources and develop service industries such as tourism.

TOURISM

For many years, Nigeria has neglected its tourism sector. But, in an attempt to bring in foreign revenue, the Nigerian government has planned and organised a new carnival in the capital Abuja. Politicians are also looking at other cultural festivals that could be developed as part of a tourism calendar.

The government wants to create a positive cultural event to attract tourists and improve the image of Nigeria abroad. However, its notorious reputation for corruption will have to be cleaned up before any significant numbers of tourists will visit Nigeria.

The manufacture of concrete blocks near Kano is typical of the small-scale manufacturing and industrial sector found across much of Nigeria.

REASONS FOR POVERTY

It is difficult to pinpoint a single reason why Nigeria's economy is quite as poor as it is. The reasons are many, complicated and often connected to each other. But most people believe the main causes are related to corruption, government mismanagement, ethnic rivalries and an over-dependence on oil. These have all led to a negative image of Nigeria abroad that has discouraged foreign investments.

CONFLICT

Since independence, Nigeria has had a succession of military governments, most of which have been toppled by a coup. Often these overthrows of the government have been violent and leaders and their followers have been assassinated. The coups have been the result of rivalries between different ethnic and religious groups, particularly the north versus the south. Against an unstable background like this, long-term planning has been impossible and Nigeria is still seen as a politically unstable country by potential overseas investors.

CORRUPTION

Government corruption became widespread during the oil boom and has continued. Political contracts were awarded to friends and family rather than being earnt. Huge amounts of money went missing as military dictators sent abroad millions of petro-dollars (income paid to oil-producing countries and deposited in Western banks). This again did not inspire confidence in Nigeria abroad. Today, politicians are still being accused of spending more time debating how much to give themselves in allowances than discussing how the country should be run.

MISPLACED PROFITS

While Nigeria does benefit from oil revenues, most of the exploration and extraction of oil is done by foreign-owned companies who take a large percentage of the profits. Nigeria does not have the capital to extract sufficient oil

High unemployment means that many people must rely on the informal economy, such as this family selling mangoes.

A worker for Shell Oil checks drilling equipment at Soku in the Niger Delta.

itself. Profits are also made from refining the oil, but Nigeria has only four, inefficient, refineries in place.

In effect, Nigeria has a dual economy. Whilst there is the lucrative oil industry operating on the world stage, the vast majority of the workforce are still engaged in subsistence agriculture and are very poor. Instead of people getting richer because of oil, they have become poorer as they face lower salaries and higher prices.

OVER-DEPENDENCE

As we have seen, Nigeria's economy is very fragile because it depends so heavily on oil. Oil accounts for almost half of Nigeria's GDP (gross domestic product) and about 90 per cent of all foreign exchange earnings. Although the country is a member of OPEC (the Organisation of Petroleum Exporting Countries), which sets the price for oil on the world market, it has little say in this and each price rise or fall affects Nigeria considerably.

DEBT

Underlying all of these problems, Nigeria's severe debt remains. The interest rates on its loans are so high that it seems unlikely they will ever be repaid. Nigeria is therefore locked in a cycle of poverty. It needs money to invest in the education and welfare of its people, to ensure an effective workforce that will contribute to the economy. However, dwindling oil revenues prevent this kind of spending.

CASE STUDY
SANI ABACHA

Sani Abacha was the President of Nigeria up until his death in 1998. He came to power through a military coup and was accused of abusing many human rights. He imprisoned those who opposed him, and in 1995 had the writer Ken Saro-Wiwa executed (see page 35). Saro-Wiwa had been campaigning against the government's support for oil companies who were polluting the Niger Delta and denying the Ogoni people a share of the oil revenues. It is believed that Abacha stashed billions of dollars in foreign bank accounts. He spent the money on himself, his family and a group of his friends. Meanwhile, ordinary Nigerians were suffering great hardships. He is remembered with a sense of shame by most Nigerians.

Sani Abacha was perhaps Nigeria's most oppressive military dictator.

STANDARDS OF LIVING

Millions of ordinary Nigerians have to live with the consequences of the failing economy and the huge cuts in government spending. Over recent years they have seen their quality of life deteriorate rapidly. The vast majority of Nigerians struggle to make ends meet. Nigeria now ranks among the lowest in the world in terms of human development.

In many ways, urban Nigeria has the outward signs of a developed, modern country – there are office blocks, hospitals, universities and hard-surfaced roads – but a look below the surface shows that appearances can be misleading. Much of the country's infrastructure is falling apart. Transport systems and buildings that were built in the 1970s are now falling into disrepair.

TRANSPORT – GOING NOWHERE

In the 1980s, Nigeria had one of the best-developed transportation systems in Africa, but it has failed to maintain it. Roads, dangerously full of potholes, are regularly the scenes of fatal accidents. In the 1990s, Nigeria had the highest road-death rate in the world, with an average of 161 deaths for every 1,000 vehicles (the UK had 2 per 1,000 vehicles). Travelling to work, particularly in cities such as Lagos and Ibadan, is very difficult – as is visiting friends and family in rural villages.

Urban congestion or 'go-slows' can make city travel slow and difficult.

TRANSPORT

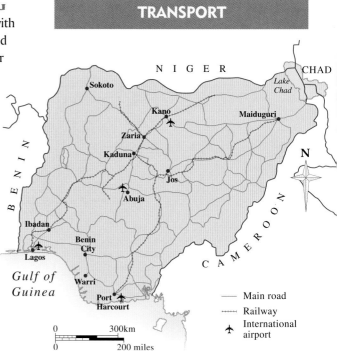

Nigeria's railways are slow, very old fashioned and highly inefficient. They were largely developed by the British during colonial years, and have since deteriorated. Relatively cheap petrol and the huge second-hand car market in Nigeria make travel by car much more affordable for local people. Trains are now hardly used at all and where they are it is mainly for freight, such as distributing fertiliser during the crop-planting season.

DECLINING URBAN SERVICES

Although most Nigerians who live in towns have electricity and running water, the supplies are erratic and frequently down. Power cuts regularly plunge people into darkness and rob factories of valuable production time, hence the National Electric Power Authority (NEPA) has been dubbed 'Never Ever Power Always'. The power cuts often occur because of corrupt officials who skim funds from the electricity budget, and because the electricity infrastructure has been allowed to deteriorate to the point where the system can no longer cope with demand.

Many Nigerians do not have access to basic primary healthcare because it is either too expensive or unavailable.

LACK OF HEALTHCARE

The implementation of the Structural Adjustment Programme in the late 1980s – the scheme imposed on Nigeria so that it could pay back its debts – led to decreased spending on social programmes. As a result, most Nigerians – especially those in rural areas – do not have access to basic primary healthcare. There is no free health service, nor are there affordable insurance schemes. What is more, in many rural areas healthcare facilities simply do not exist. Here, people still rely on traditional medicines or simply do without. The hospitals and clinics in urban areas are available only to the wealthy.

Unofficial medicine sellers are a common sight on Nigerian streets – they offer cheap remedies, but relatively few of them have any proper medical training. Diseases arising from poor sanitation and malnutrition, as well as the high risk of HIV (see page 55), put many Nigerians in a very dangerous position.

STRUGGLING TO LEARN

Nigerians put a great value on education and many receive a decent schooling. But families struggle and make enormous sacrifices to pay for the uniforms and books their children need. It is quite common for children to have to drop out of school to work, in order to help the family survive. In rural areas, many children stay at home during peak periods of the agricultural cycle to help out on the farm. Even those people who have received a good education cannot always find work. For secondary school graduates there is an unemployment rate of 35 to 40 per cent.

SHARING THE WEALTH?

Resentment has built up among Nigerians who can see the potential for wealth that oil could bring, but who know that the vast majority of the population are missing out. The oil industry has become the target for some of their anger. Pipelines have been sabotaged and oil installations attacked by young people demanding that the oil wealth be used for everyone's benefit. It is believed that local people sometimes sabotage pipelines to create jobs for themselves, since they know that the oil companies will hire them to clean up the oil spills afterwards.

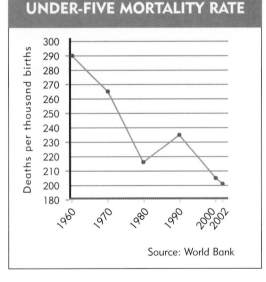

UNDER-FIVE MORTALITY RATE

Source: World Bank

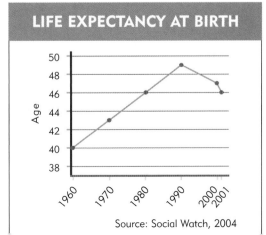

LIFE EXPECTANCY AT BIRTH

Source: Social Watch, 2004

Most people in Nigeria still depend on fuelwood for household energy.

Nigeria is a country with considerable biodiversity – in other words, it has a rich range of natural environments, animals and plants. There are mangrove swamps, savannahs, rainforests, deserts and mountainous areas, with many different species of flora and fauna.

Unfortunately, Nigeria's ecology is under threat as the growing population, grinding poverty, unplanned development and climate change cause increasing damage. However, the government now recognises that there is a problem and is taking measures to protect the environment.

THE RAINFORESTS

Rainforests are important, wherever they are in the world, because they support many different types of animals and plants. They are often referred to as 'the lungs of the world' because trees and plants return oxygen to the atmosphere. In fact, rainforests are one of the world's most precious resources. But they are

Roads through the rainforest provide commercial logging trucks with access to hardwood timber.

Exposed topsoil around Laminga is easily eroded by heavy rain.

cover only 15 per cent of the country's total land area. In the more densely populated areas, many trees have been cleared to make way for cocoa and rubber plantations. Parts of the forest have also been destroyed for road building. Clearing the land leaves the topsoil exposed to heavy rainfall and leads to gullying and erosion, making the land useless for farming of any kind.

DESERTIFICATION

Desertification is a major problem in Nigeria. Around the towns of Sokoto, Kano and Katsina in the north, much of the vegetation has been removed by continuous cropping, overgrazing and bush burning. Together with drought, this has led to a process of desertification, whereby an area of land becomes like a desert. First of all trees disappear, and finally grasses and bushes give way to expansive areas of desert-like sand. Some people talk about the gradual southward sprawl of the Sahara Desert. The situation has been worsened by massive irrigation schemes, as water is diverted from already dry areas. This is considered to be one of the most serious problems facing the northern states of Nigeria, which are important agricultural areas. It could have grave consequences for the whole nation.

also valued for the commercial logging of hardwood timbers such as mahogany and iroko, used for making furniture. There is a real danger that if Nigeria's rainforests continue to be felled at the rate they have been, they will soon vanish altogether.

Already between 70 and 80 per cent of the original forests have disappeared, and they now

CASE STUDY
FARMING IN THE NORTH

Hassan Mohamed followed in his father's footsteps and became a commercial groundnut farmer in northern Nigeria. He also grew food crops for his family to eat. When he started farming, the soils were fertile and the rains reliable. At harvest time the family were able to sell some of their surplus food at the local market.

However, in the early 1980s a decade of drought began. This resulted in crop failure and the death of livestock. Large sections of

land that had been fertile were increasingly invaded by sand dunes. Hassan and his family were stricken by poverty; some of their neighbours moved to cities further south. Hassan noticed that because many trees had been cut down, allowing water to run off the surface, the level of groundwater had dropped and the local streams and rivers were much shallower than they had been. Life has changed a lot for Hassan and his family and things are much more difficult for them today than they were 20 years ago. Hassan is no longer able to earn a living from farming and takes casual employment whenever he can find it.

THREATS OF DEVELOPMENT

Before modern development, Nigeria's diverse habitats of mangrove swamps, tropical rainforests, savannah and mountain plateaux supported many different species of plants and animals. However, over the last few decades, vast areas of natural habitat have been taken over by land degradation, the building of towns and cities to house the rapidly growing population, industrial developments and the expansion of farmland. The homes of thousands of species of plants and animals have been destroyed.

WETLANDS AT RISK

Nigeria's rivers and lakes have fared badly under development. Wetland habitats (or *fadama* lands), which are home to many species of birds and animals, have been cleared for irrigation. Their flood-dependent ecosystems have been damaged by dam construction, which has upset the natural cycle of flooding. For example, the Jere Bowl – a previously important rice-producing area which depended on seasonal flooding – has been badly affected by a dam built in the 1980s under a multi-million-dollar World Bank urban water supply project.

The largest tract of mangroves in Africa – and the third-largest in the world – is contained in the Niger Delta region. Areas like this are important as fish nurseries where fish can breed. Furthermore, the mangrove plants act as buffers against erosion by waves – when the mangroves are removed, the land is easily and quickly eroded. But the Delta is also under threat from oil pollution, the removal of sand for construction materials and overfishing. Over 40 per cent of Nigeria's mangrove swamps have already been lost.

ENDANGERED ANIMALS

The widespread hunting of wildlife for food has increasingly threatened the animal population. Many once-common species are now found only in very remote areas or inside major reserves and game parks. These include Nigeria's few remaining elephants – which were hunted for the ivory from their tusks – buffalos, lions, leopards and other large game. Smaller animals such as antelope, monkeys, jackals and hyenas, are still found and are quite widespread. Hippopotamuses and crocodiles also remain fairly common in the largest rivers. Birds, including species that migrate seasonally between Africa and Europe, are abundant. However, some species, such as the grey parrot, are illegally exported to countries such as Saudi Arabia and could become endangered. The grey parrot is popular for its ability to mimic speech.

Leaking oil pipelines have caused large-scale environmental degradation in the fragile ecosystems of the Delta.

The Ogoni people consist of about 500,000 Nigerians who live and work on or near the Niger Delta in the south of the country. They came to the attention of the world in 1995 when nine leading Ogoni campaigners, including the writer Ken Saro-Wiwa, were executed by the government. The Ogoni have long struggled against the oil company Shell for exploiting their land. Their farming areas and fishing grounds have been polluted by oil leaks, depriving them of their livelihoods. They also suffered severe repression under the military regimes, who were determined to ensure that this major oil company did not leave Nigeria. The Movement for the Survival of Ogoni People – an organisation representing their cause – campaigns for better access to oil profits.

This man is standing by what used to be a natural spring that supplied his village in Ogoniland with water. The spring was destroyed when an oil pipeline burst in the mid-1970s.

OIL AND GAS POLLUTION

Pollution from oil activities in the Niger Delta is a serious environmental problem. Some of this is by way of oil spills which contaminate the land and ruin it for farming and fishing. There have been more than 4,000 oil spills since 1960. But there is also air pollution from the burning of excess gas that comes up with the crude oil. This is known as gas flaring. It produces methane, which has more potential to create global warming than the carbon dioxide given off by cars and factories.

URBAN POLLUTION

Serious environmental problems are caused by the unplanned development of city areas in Nigeria. Lagos, for example, grew up so rapidly that there was no time, money or organisation to ensure that an adequate sewerage system was in place (see page 45). Consequently, the haphazard streets – crammed with makeshift homes – are lined with unhealthy open sewers. The volume of cars, congested roads, and the heat, all contribute to a fog of pollution – 'smog' – that hangs over the city on most days.

Industrial waste and polythene bag pollution are other serious environmental hazards that many Nigerian cities share. Nigeria is a major producer of polythene bags, which are often discarded after use. As there are no proper waste disposal or recycling facilities, the bags litter the landscape. They accumulate in waterways and block drains, causing stagnant water to gather, which provides a breeding ground for diseases.

Human sewage is a common pollutant of drainage channels in the slum dwellings around Lagos.

SAVING THE ENVIRONMENT

Since Nigeria's return to democracy in 1999, there has been a renewed interest and concern for the environment by both the government and campaigning groups. The government, despite its lack of funds, is attempting to address some of the environmental problems the country faces. There are several active environmental campaigning groups in Nigeria putting pressure on politicians to do even more.

TRADITIONAL METHODS

There is an increased interest in traditional methods of farming, which people now realise were very effective ways of conserving the land. These methods have been used for centuries. They include planting different crops all at the same time, in the same field, to ensure an even coverage that binds the soil. This is known as 'intercropping'. It reduces erosion and also makes the soil more fertile. In areas such as the Jos Plateau, where there are areas of steep land, farmers have built terraces that prevent soil creep and make the best use of valuable land.

Many traditional methods are very effective for preserving and using water efficiently. Earth dams, for example, are built to harvest and store water during the short rainy season in the north. The water is then used for irrigation and the reclamation of degraded farmlands.

REFORESTATION

Replanting trees helps to counteract several environmental problems. It provides habitats for animals and secures the topsoil, preventing erosion and subsequently recharging and replacing groundwater. The government is aiming to replace forest cover by banning the export of timber, promoting the replanting of forests and encouraging local communities to develop their own conservation schemes. In the north, acacia trees and vetiva grass are being planted to prevent and minimise the possible effects of erosion and the advance of sand dunes.

Maigatari tree nursery produces seedlings that are distributed to help combat desertification and provide an income.

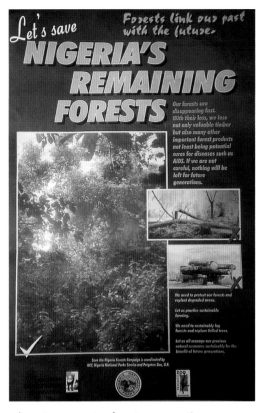

A poster promotes forest conservation. Finding the balance between local needs and conservation is a great challenge.

Cross River state in eastern Nigeria has an exceptionally diverse and rich range of habitats and species. It is the home of several species of primates – such as gorillas, baboons and chimpanzees – migratory and resident birds, and more than 950 types of butterfly. Many of Africa's rarest trees, such as mahogany, ironwood, camwood and mimosup, are found here – but exports of these to Europe, America and Japan have been seriously depleting the forests. In the Cross River National Park, scientists do regular biodiversity surveys to monitor changes. They also consult with the Efik, Ejagham and the Bekwarra people who live in the forest and have developed a vast knowledge of the ecology over hundreds of years. In an attempt to stop the destruction of this valuable forest area, the state's governor has suspended all licences permitting logging.

Baboons are one of the many protected species in Cross River National Park.

There are also a number of successful government 'shelterbelt' projects in the north of the country – in Jigawa state, for example. Trees are planted in strips or 'belts', about 30m across, to act as wind barriers and reduce soil erosion on the farms alongside them. Most often, it is the *neem* tree, a species imported from India, that is used because of its ability to withstand harsh environments.

NATIONAL PARKS AND RESERVES

Nigeria has a system of national parks and reserves, where the aim is to protect and conserve the natural environment and wildlife. Elephants, hippopotamuses and antelopes can be seen in game reserves such as Kainji and Birnin Gwari. Gorillas, thought no longer to exist in the country, have recently been found in the dense forests of the south-east.

Nigeria cooperates with neighbouring Cameroon, Chad and Niger to manage the wildlife in areas around their common borders.

POPULATION AND SETTLEMENT

Large families are common and children often provide a valuable supply of rural labour.

Nigeria's enormous population – the largest in Africa – is one of the things for which it is most famous and which gives it the title 'the Giant of Africa'. In 2004, the population was estimated at over 137 million.

POPULATION GROWTH

Nigeria's population is growing rapidly – at about 3 per cent per year. Some experts predict that by the year 2025, 206 million people will be living there. The population is growing so fast because there is a very high birth rate – approximately 40.16 births per 1,000 people. Each woman gives birth, on average, six times in her lifetime. The death rate is comparatively low, at 13.72 per 1,000, despite increasing fatalities due to HIV/AIDS (see page 55). Infant mortality rates are falling but are still high. It is unheard of, and considered very unlucky, to name a child before it is born as so many die during childbirth and in infancy.

FAMILY SIZE

In 1988, the government put forward the National Population Policy. This was aimed at reducing population growth. It encouraged women to have fewer children and promoted the health and welfare of mothers and children to improve their quality of life. It recommended that couples should have no more than four children per family. But the policy failed. A large family is highly valued and seen as a status symbol in Nigeria. Having children is also important in a society where many infants die, and where extending the family is the best way to ensure that you will be cared for when you are old. Many farming

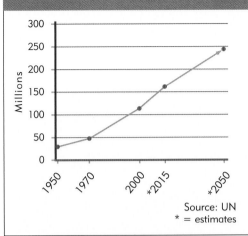

Millions

Source: UN
* = estimates

for many years. The number of people in each ethnic group determines how many seats they are awarded in the House of Representatives (Nigeria's parliament) and therefore how much power they have in the government. There have been accusations in the past that censuses have been manipulated by one or other of the different ethnic groups, to show that it has a majority of the population. A census in 1973 claimed that 64 per cent of the population lived in the north, but this census was disallowed.

STRAINED SERVICES

Despite cuts in education funding, most Nigerians are well educated and skilled. This creates a strong labour force. Another strength is that Nigeria has a vast internal market – there are lots of people to buy manufactured consumer products and pay for services. However, on the downside is the fact that such a vast population needs to be fed, and to have certain basic social and welfare provisions. These are things that the government is hard-pressed to provide.

families also prefer to have many children so that there is adequate labour to help on the farm. Nearly half of all Nigerians are younger than 15 years old. The average life expectancy is just 46 years.

POPULATION DENSITY

Nigeria's large population is not evenly distributed throughout the country. Some urban areas are very densely populated, with as many as 1,000 people per square kilometre. These include cities such as Kano and Lagos. In the rural, arid areas of the north, densities are well below 50 people per square kilometre. However, not all rural areas are sparsely populated. In parts of the countryside around Kano it is estimated that there are more than 140 people per square kilometre. Some rural areas in the south also experience relatively high densities. This means that a lot of pressure is put on basic resources such as land for farming, water and fuelwood.

POPULATION ISSUES

Nigeria's vast population is both one of its strengths and one of its weaknesses. Various issues arise from the population's diversity and size.

ETHNIC CONFLICT

The exact size and proportion of the different ethnic groups within Nigeria has been a matter of great political controversy

POPULATION STRUCTURE, 2004

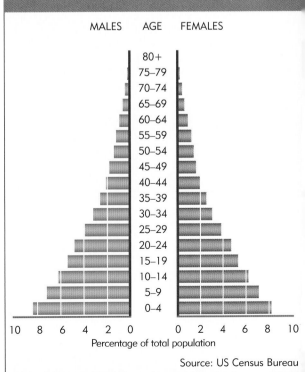

MALES   AGE   FEMALES

Percentage of total population

Source: US Census Bureau

URBANISATION

Urbanisation refers to the changes that take place in a country when the number of people living in cities and towns increases. In 1991, about 36 per cent of Nigeria's population lived in urban areas. This has now increased to almost half the population, creating what is known as 'urban bias'.

People – particularly those who have had an education – leave the countryside to look for work in the cities. The factor that pulls them to the cities is the prospect of work and the expectation of a more exciting life. The factors that push them away from the countryside are

Services such as electricity, clean water and sewage disposal often do not exist in shanty towns such as this.

the scarcity of land, and the poor soils leading to declining crop yields. It is usually the young, particularly young men, who go to the cities in search of a better standard of living.

PROBLEMS AND PATTERNS

Most of the people leaving the countryside move to huge, sprawling cities in the south – Lagos, Ibadan, Warri, Benin City and Port Harcourt, for example. The northern cities of Kano, Kaduna and Sokoto are also popular. This influx of people into towns and cities has led to the rapid and phenomenal growth of large urban centres, creating congestion, overcrowding, poor housing, poor sanitation, unemployment, poverty and crime.

The oil boom stimulated migration to cities in the south. Since then, migration has waxed and waned with the state of the economy.

Many people leave the poor soils of northern Nigeria in the hope of a better life in the cities.

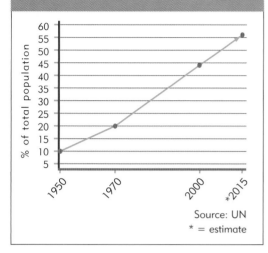

Source: UN
* = estimate

When the economy suffers a downturn and there is a shortage of jobs in the cities, migration declines and some people return to their home villages.

SEASONAL WORKERS

The improvement in roads in the 1970s meant it became feasible for workers from the north to come south. They would work as hired labourers in the cocoa belt and

elsewhere at the onset of the rains, and later return to their home villages in time to plant their own crops. The Hausa call this pattern of seasonal migration *cin rani,* which means 'eating away the dry season'. Even though roads are now dangerously neglected, labour shortages on some farms mean that migrant workers are willing to travel around the country working where they can.

THE BRAIN DRAIN

Nigeria is experiencing increased levels of emigration as those who have a good education – and can afford to leave – go abroad to live. Nearly every country in the world has a Nigerian community – Nigerian students and residents are found particularly in other parts of West Africa, the USA and the UK. In these communities, people continue with many of their traditional customs and festivals. Emigration is a problem for Nigeria as it loses some of its most able and most qualified young people to other countries. However, they often send money back to their families. Throughout Nigeria this adds up to millions of dollars each year and is a key factor in helping Nigerians set up businesses.

CASE STUDY
LEAVING FOR A BETTER LIFE

Ibrahim Olorode was born in 1967 and brought up in Ibadan in southern Nigeria. He studied accountancy at university and worked in a bank for a year. But life in Nigeria was difficult. At that time, Nigeria was still under military rule and many people did not feel free to say what they wanted. In 1996, Ibrahim left Nigeria to go to the Gambia where he worked as a teacher in a secondary school. Here he met an English woman. They married and now live in England where Ibrahim is a security guard in the offices of a large insurance company in Bristol. Ibrahim says things are better now in Nigeria under civilian rule, and he would like to return to visit his family and friends one day.

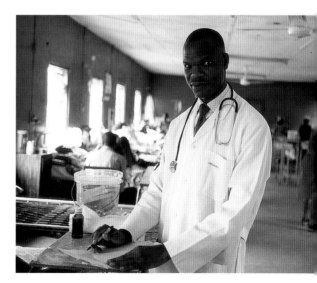

Nigeria must provide opportunities for its educated professionals if the 'brain drain' phenomenon is to be avoided.

ABOVE: A compound with traditional dwellings and buildings in a Hausa/Fulani village.

BELOW: Socialising is an important pastime, especially in village life.

RURAL NIGERIA

More than 50 per cent of Nigeria's people still live in villages and in the countryside. Life here is almost exclusively based on subsistence agriculture, although people are increasingly taking other jobs in order to afford farm inputs such as chemical fertiliser. There have been small changes in, for example, construction materials – tin is now used instead of grass for roofing – and some mechanisation of farm tools has taken place. But generally very little has altered for hundreds of years. Villages have few modern services. Women and girls usually collect water from a well or a standpipe, and more often than not there is no electricity.

EFFECTS OF URBANISATION

Rural areas have been severely affected by mass migration to the cities. The great majority of migrants are men of working age,

Osoroko-Lekki is a Yoruba village on the Lekki Peninsula, about 70km east of Lagos. It is built in the traditional Yoruba way, with houses clustered around a communal courtyard. As brothers and sons married and brought their wives to the compound, more houses were built. If there was not enough land to build another house, a new piece of land would be found and a new line of the family established.

The village is smaller than it used to be when trade in salt with people of the northern savannah was an important economic activity. The permanent population of the village is now only about 200 people. Most of the inhabitants are mothers, children and the elderly. Others have left the village for Lagos in search of paid work, but they still regard Osoroko-Lekki as their home and return for festivals and family celebrations, showing off their city clothes.

In many ways, life in the village has changed little for hundreds of years. Some villagers still live in traditional houses made from wood and grass, all obtained locally. However, in the mid-1980s, modern cement bungalows with piped water and electricity were built, mainly by people who returned briefly from their work in Lagos to build houses in preparation for their retirement. Around the village, slash and burn agriculture – where vegetation is cut down and burned to create fertile ash-based soil for planting – and the cultivation of new crops, such as cassava and cashew, have altered the environment.

Osoroko-Lekki is a typical Yoruba village on the Lekki Peninsula.

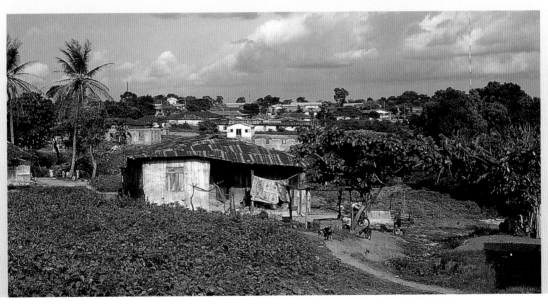

so the rural areas from which they come have been left with a population imbalance in favour of women, younger children and older people. Whereas, in the past, it was common for relatives to stay in the village to help raise children and care for the old people, the pressures of modern life are such that the extended family is breaking up and such ties can no longer be counted on.

As men leave the villages, jobs – such as weeding and harvesting – still have to be done, usually by women and children. Some are done by hired labourers who move around the country. However, sometimes there is no one to do the jobs at all and farms fall into decline and become overgrown. With the growth in the population and the increased demand for food from the cities, this is a serious problem.

NIGERIA'S CITIES

Nigeria has many very large cities, all of which have certain similarities. However, cities in the north and south have developed in different ways, which are reflected in their layout and in their architecture.

CITY STRUCTURE

Pre-colonial Yoruba cities in the south were built as a series of compounds – enclosed areas with several buildings in which one family lived.

Some wealthy Nigerians live in smart new housing estates, such as this home in the suburbs of Lagos.

These compounds were part of districts, each with their own leader. Surrounding the urban area was a forest for hunting and to provide protection. Beyond this was farmland belonging to the city dwellers. Sometimes, for instance during the planting season, city men and women would stay on their farms for several days to plant or harvest. Similarly, people living

CASE STUDY
KANO

Located in the north, at the crossroads of several cultures, Kano is one of the oldest cities in sub-Saharan Africa. It dates back over 1,000 years. Its traditional architecture reflects the influence of Islam and North Africa, with intricate and ornate patterns on walls and buildings. Kano is a classic example of a 'dual city', incorporating a bustling modern centre (Sabon Gari) – designed and built for those who came to live in Kano from the south – and an ancient walled Islamic city.

For centuries Kano has been one of the most active commercial centres in West Africa. Its leatherwork – made from goatskin – was traded in Europe as far back as the fifteenth century. Kano was also renowned for cloth dying and it is still possible to see people working at the famous dye-pits, colouring fabric in the same way as they have done for hundreds of years.

Kano's dye-pits date back hundreds of years and remain an interesting aspect of the city today.

Today, Kano is Nigeria's third-largest city. Cotton textiles, steel furniture, processed meats, concrete blocks, indigo dye and shoes are now manufactured here, and cotton and cattle are traded and shipped elsewhere.

in surrounding villages often had property in the town and considered that they belonged to the town. They divided their time between the town and the village. This close relationship between urban areas and the surrounding rural areas remains in many Yoruba cities today.

The cities in the north were historically centres of power and developed as city states, extracting taxes from areas under their control.

THE CAPITAL CITY

Lagos used to be the capital of Nigeria. But in 1976 it was decided to move the capital to Abuja. This new city was built in the centre of the country, to try to bring an end to the ethnic troubles of the past by favouring neither north nor south. Abuja was built on land independent of any ethnic or religious group, and its central location was to be a symbol of greater cooperation between all Nigerians. It officially became Nigeria's capital in 1991 and is the base of the central government. In 2004, peace talks were held there, aimed at finding a solution to western Sudan's Darfur crisis (a bloody conflict between the Arab government and rebel black African groups).

CASE STUDY
LAGOS

Lagos, on Lagos Island, was established in the fifteenth century. It began as a trading post between the Benin kingdom and Portuguese traders, exporting ivory, peppers and slaves. When Nigeria fell into the hands of the British, they began exporting food crops.

The heart of Lagos is the area known as Eko. This is where the commercial and administrative headquarters of the city are. It is linked to the mainland by three bridges, and to Ikoyi and Victoria Island by road. These are the residential areas where richer Nigerians live.

But most of the city is the result of rapid, haphazard building that started in the early 1970s. Thousands of people moved here from the countryside. At the same time, refugees and migrants from

Lagos epitomises many of the problems that many large African cities face, including crime, unemployment, pollution and urban sprawl.

other African countries arrived. It is now a chaotic, dirty city that consumes 45 per cent of Nigeria's energy. Much of the housing is below standard and the sewerage system is inadequate. Traffic is extremely heavy and it can take two to three hours to travel 15km across the city. The crime rate in Lagos is particularly high, with car-jackings and burglaries high on the list of offences. Rich Lagos residents – who may have something to steal – live in high-security compounds equipped with razor-wire fencing and patrolled by armed guards.

Christian church services, such as this one in Lagos, are important community social events.

With more than 250 different ethnic groups, Nigeria is a complex cultural mix. It reflects both African and Islamic traditions, and more recently – and to a lesser extent – Western influences.

RELIGION

Nigeria's main religions are Islam and Christianity. Some people still follow traditional religions, such as animism – the belief that natural objects such as trees and rocks are inhabited by powerful spirits – and often these beliefs are incorporated into the main religions.

In the north, the Hausa and Fulani people are mainly Muslim and make up about half the population. This means that Nigeria has one of the largest communities of Muslims in the world. The Yoruba and Igbo in the south, making up 40 per cent of the population, are mainly Christian although some are Muslim.

Unfortunately religion is one of the major factors that divides Nigerians. It has been the cause of serious outbreaks of violence in recent years. In 2000, Islamic Sharia Law was

A mosque in Abuja. The city was built on land independent of any religious group, and now Christians and Muslims live there side by side.

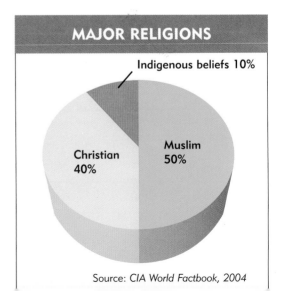

MAJOR RELIGIONS

Indigenous beliefs 10%

Christian 40%

Muslim 50%

Source: *CIA World Factbook, 2004*

This classroom in Ibadan illustrates the poor conditions and overcrowding that are typical of most Nigerian schools.

introduced by some northern states – largely as a response to Westernisation and to reinforce the Islamic way of life. Sharia Law makes certain activities – such as adultery – criminal offences, and strict punishment is applied. Many non-Muslims who live in these states object to Sharia Law, creating much conflict.

LANGUAGE

It is estimated that more than 500 different languages are spoken in Nigeria. Some of these are understood by only a few hundred people. On the islands of the Delta region, there are villages only a few kilometres apart where people speak completely different languages – so different that they are incomprehensible to each other.

Children in schools are taught in English, which is also used in government, businesses and the media, although nearly everyone speaks their own language at home. Nigerians think nothing of being able to speak three or more languages. A form of 'pidgin-English' is widely spoken throughout the south of the country, similar to the 'pidgin' spoken in Liberia and Sierra Leone, where it is called Krio.

EDUCATION

Education, particularly Western-style education, is seen as a way of gaining a better job and income and greater status in society. In rural areas, children learn skills from their family or on the job as a kind of apprentice, either in addition to or instead of going to school.

Levels of education are highest in the south. This is generally thought to be due to Western-style teaching, which was introduced to Nigeria by (and associated with) Christian missionaries. In the north, many Muslim people are still suspicious of Western education, because they feel that there is a hidden agenda to dilute the Islamic religion. Thus many traditional families in the north choose to send their children to Muslim Koranic (or Qur'anic) schools, where they are taught in Arabic.

FAMILY LIFE

In Nigeria, as in many other African countries, the family unit is still relatively strong and a powerful sense of community exists. Extended families – where several generations of a family live together – are common, especially in rural areas. Older people are particularly well respected. Nigerians are often shocked when they hear that people in Western countries allow their elderly parents to live in residential homes, rather than take care of them themselves. However, things are changing now and the pressures of modern life sometimes mean that the ties binding the extended family are loosening.

CASE STUDY
THE ORAL TRADITION

In Nigeria, as in other parts of Africa, people developed a way of passing on their history by word of mouth. Much of the history of a family or ethnic group is learnt through stories or poems that explain the history of their ancestors. These are then passed down and added to through the generations. In northern Nigeria, due to the frequent droughts, the subject of much Hausa oral history is 'feast and famine'. Talking drums – held under the arm and played with a stick – are a traditional form of communication in rural areas. They are used as an imitation of speech, to convey messages from one village to another, and to recite history and sing praises to the chief.

Weddings are major financial responsibilities, and families must plan for them years in advance.

LITERATURE AND COMMUNICATION

Nigerians are avid readers of newspapers and listeners to the radio. They like to know what is going on in the world and enjoy debating and arguing about topical issues. There are many different daily newspapers, most in English but some in local languages such as Yoruba and Hausa.

Many Nigerian writers have gained world recognition for their novels and poems. Chinua Achebe wrote about the effects of colonial rule on traditional ways of life. Wole Soyinka has written poetry, plays, novels and non-fiction and was awarded the Nobel Prize for Literature in 1986.

CELEBRATIONS AND FESTIVALS

In Nigeria there is always an excuse to have a party, and both Christian and Muslim festivals are celebrated to the full. Christmas Day, Boxing Day, Good Friday, and New Year's Day – as well as *Eid-al-Fitr* (the end of Ramadan), *Eid-al-Kabir* and *Eid-al-Maulud* – are all national holidays.

The Islamic festivals in northern Nigeria are spectacular occasions when brightly dressed men on decorated horses take part in processions, followed by wrestlers and musicians.

Regattas and fishing festivals also take place. The famous Argungu festival in Sokoto is a very popular attraction. Hundreds of fishermen dive into the river and emerge a short while later with fish they have caught in their bare hands. Many festivals are related to the harvesting of crops, such as the Yam Festival in the south-east.

Weddings and naming ceremonies are lively events often attended by hundreds of people. The music, dancing and feasting can last for several days. Even funerals are cause for celebration – many people believe that death means joining the ancestors, so the deceased must be given a good send-off. However, these ceremonies are often major financial obligations and Nigerians must plan years in advance to pay for them.

ART

Islamic influences are to be seen in the arts, especially in the architecture of the north. However, Islam does not allow the representation of people and animals in art forms, so ceremonial carvings are virtually absent in Muslim states. The National Museum in Lagos has a rich collection of art from all periods. The Nigerian government has sought to prevent the removal of significant Nigerian art from the country and to return art taken abroad during the colonial era.

CRAFTS

Woodcarving is the most common form of artistic expression, especially among those who live in the south. Ebony (which is black) and white wood are most often used. The ancestral and ceremonial woodcarvings of the Benin, Igbo, Ibibio and Yoruba craftsmen are among the most beautiful works of art.

Traditional textiles include embroidery, weaving, *adire* (tie-dye) and silk-screen printing. *Adire* is traditionally associated with the Abeokuta, Ibadan and Osogbo peoples, but modern designs using *adire* are found in other states in Nigeria. Leatherwork, metalwork, glass beadwork, raffia and grass weaving and calabash carving (a calabash is a type of gourd) are popular in different parts of the country.

Drumming is a popular pastime, and also an important part of Nigerian culture.

MUSIC

Music is the driving force of any occasion or event in Nigeria. It is central to the way Nigerians celebrate and express themselves. Songs and dances are played on drums, flutes, trumpets, stringed instruments, xylophones and thumb pianos. Music is an integral part of receptions, marriages, naming ceremonies and even job promotions.

Traditional and modern music are both widespread. Pop music can be heard in the nightclubs of the cities and towns and on the radio. 'Highlife' and 'Juju' bands mix Western music with African beats and instruments. Famous Highlife artists are King Sunny Ade and Ebenezer Obe. Lagos is the most important city for modern music in West Africa, and musicians come from all over Africa to perform here.

This leather craftsman in Zaria continues to work using centuries-old traditional methods.

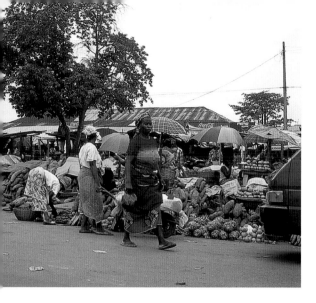

FOOD

Traditional Nigerian food is based on local produce such as vegetables, meat and fish. It is cooked into stews and soups and eaten with rice, cassava or yam. But in the cities fast food, such as burgers, and food from street vendors, such as deep-fried beancakes, is increasingly popular. Bread has become an urban staple.

A widely eaten dish is boiled yam, which is pounded to make something similar to mashed potatoes. This is called *fu-fu* and is eaten with a vegetable, meat or fish stew. Rice is commonly cooked with ground tomatoes, peppers and meat or fish. Palm oil is a thick, rich, reddish-brown oil made from ground palm kernels and is often used in cooking. Some Nigerian food is cooked in hot chilli sauce. In the north, *tuwo* is the staple food, made from rice or the flour of millet or sorghum. It is cooked in boiling water and stirred until thick, then served with a spicy sauce or soup.

MEALTIMES

At mealtimes, people gather round one bowl and eat with their hand or a spoon. Even soup may be eaten with the hand. Men usually dine separately from women and children. Visitors are always invited to share a meal as hospitality is at the heart of the Nigerian lifestyle.

Fast food has become increasingly popular in Nigeria, although many takeaway restaurants still serve traditional dishes.

LEISURE

Nigeria has a long tradition of theatre. Plays are often based on biblical stories, comedies, political satires and protests. Cinema is increasingly popular and Nigeria has its own film industry known as 'Nollywood', producing films that are distributed all over West Africa.

At the weekends people enjoy going to watch a wrestling match, or they play *ayoby yor* – a traditional board game using seeds or stones. Marbles, skipping, clapping and singing games and flying kites are all popular with children. Wealthy Nigerians living in the urban areas often belong to sports clubs and gyms, but these are inaccessible to most people.

SPORT

Nigerians are mad about sport. Just about every sport you can think of is played in Nigeria, including basketball and baseball, golf and tennis – but football (soccer) is the most popular by far. The national team is called the Super Eagles and several members also play for UK and European sides, where salaries are high. Nigeria's team won the gold medal in the 1996 Olympics in Atlanta and in 2002 they qualified for the World Cup finals. Nigeria also has a national women's football team that has

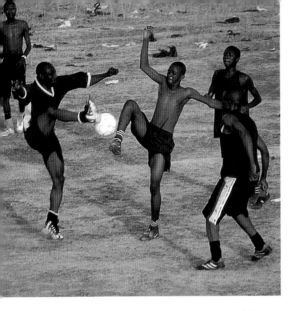

Football is the most widely followed sport in Nigeria, and it is one of the country's great passions.

TELEVISION SETS (PER 1,000 PEOPLE)

Source: World Bank

participated in the Olympic Games. Several Nigerians have moved to the USA and Canada to compete professionally in sports such as basketball and boxing.

Athletics is another sport at which Nigerians excel and where they have achieved success at international level – particularly the 100m and 200m sprint events. Wrestling is a traditional Yoruba sport which has a big following.

MOBILE PHONES

The growth in the use of mobile phones in Africa as a whole and in Nigeria in particular has been phenomenal. The old fixed landline system was so poor that people have welcomed mobile phones with open arms. For most Nigerians, a mobile is the first phone they have ever owned, owing to the huge expense and poor availability of landline phones.

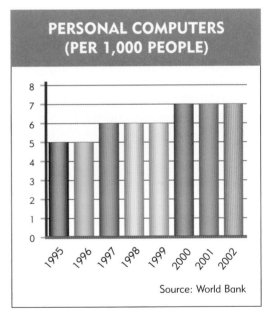

PERSONAL COMPUTERS (PER 1,000 PEOPLE)

Source: World Bank

TELECOMMUNICATIONS DATA (PER 1,000 PEOPLE)

Mainline Phones	6
Mobile Phones	13
Internet Users	3

Source: World Bank, 2002

Nigerians are great talkers and mobile phones allow them to stay in touch with their family and friends. They have become the most important means of communication. The average length of time that each mobile phone is used in a week in Nigeria is 200 minutes, compared to 120 in Britain and 88 in Germany. This is because mobile phones are often shared between several people. Some people set up businesses on street corners, offering their phones to customers willing to pay by the minute to make a call.

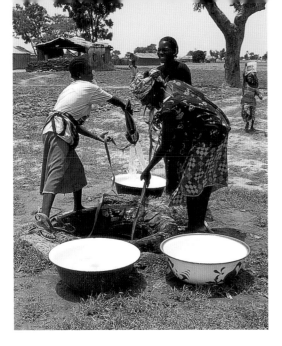

Collecting water from wells is one of the many tasks that women must undertake.

WOMEN IN NIGERIA

Nigerian women have always played an important role in the family and in society. They are expected to be the wage earners in the family, and they do most of the farming, as well as fishing, herding and trade. They are also the mainstays of family and cultural life, and are playing an increasing role in business and politics.

Women do up to 80 per cent of the farming in Nigeria and produce two-thirds of the food crops. This is in addition to their household chores of fetching water, cooking and looking after children. They often spend up to 16 hours a day working.

In every town in Nigeria there is a market. Women go there to buy food and to sell any surplus produce they may have. They are also places where women can meet each other and catch up with the latest gossip. They are colourful, lively and noisy places, with much chattering and bargaining going on.

In order to make extra money, women do jobs such as hairdressing, soap making or mat weaving. They often get together as cooperatives, to help each other profit. For instance, sometimes they set up savings schemes whereby they all put in a certain amount of money each week and take it in turns to borrow the money. This enables them to pay for expensive items, such as a sewing machine or some chickens, or to set up a small business.

Women are responsible for much of the household and farm work. These women near Kano are weeding their sorghum plot.

WOMEN AND ISLAM

In the north, where most people are Muslims, men are allowed to have more than one wife. In homes where there are no mod cons, this can make life easier for women as they can share the chores. The custom of keeping women separate from the rest of society and covered with head-to-toe clothing, known as purdah, prevents women from taking part in many social and political activities.

The Islamic Sharia Law (see page 47) has brought in new rules and punishments, many of which affect women more than men. One Islamic court ruled that a woman found guilty of adultery should be stoned to death, but there was an international outcry and the decision was reversed. Separate schools for girls and single-sex taxis are other features of this gender discrimination.

These girls are wearing *hijabs*, part of the traditional Islamic dress.

WOMEN AND CHILDREN

Given the option, the majority of Nigerian women would choose to have fewer children. They are among the most likely women in the world to die because of complications during pregnancy. Midwives, town criers and village health providers are involved in education about family planning, and the use of contraception among married women aged 15 to 49 years has increased from 3 to 15 per cent in some parts of Nigeria.

If the family is short of money, it is likely that girls will be forced to leave school rather than boys. In an attempt to redress this, schools are opening especially for women who have missed out on education.

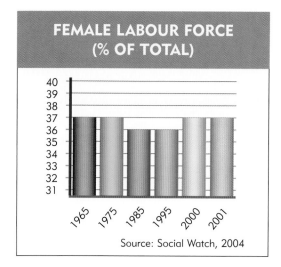

FEMALE LABOUR FORCE (% OF TOTAL)

Source: Social Watch, 2004

CASE STUDY
THE MISS WORLD CONTROVERSY

In 2002, the Miss World beauty contest was to be held in Abuja, the capital of Nigeria. Many Muslims were unhappy about this because they believe that parading women in this way is immoral and against their religion. When a Nigerian journalist wrote a newspaper article claiming that the prophet Mohammed would have approved, thousands took to the streets of the northern city of Kaduna in protest. They burnt churches and looted shops and more than 100 people were killed. The contest was hurriedly moved to the UK. Meanwhile, the journalist involved (herself a woman) became the subject of a *fatwa* – a religious order calling for her death – by the government of Zamfara state. She was forced into hiding.

Inequality is a major problem in Nigeria. This businessman is wealthy, but most of the population remains poor.

N igeria stands at a crossroads. A famous Nigerian author, Chinua Achebe, once claimed that Nigeria was one of the most disorderly nations in the world. It certainly faces huge challenges, but the potential to develop into a thriving, productive and wealthy nation still remains. Certain hurdles have to be overcome, however, before that can happen.

TACKLING POVERTY

Poverty is still a growing problem in Nigeria despite the estimated US$280 billion earned from oil since the 1970s. According to the World Bank, about 66 per cent of the population now live below the poverty line, compared to 43 per cent in 1985. The reality of this is that prices of basic goods are rising dramatically, and incidences of malnutrition are increasing, especially amongst children. This situation is particularly bad in the extreme north-east and north-west, where significant numbers of children suffer from rickets and are undernourished. Growing poverty and the huge gap between the rich and the poor is a source of unrest. Finding a solution is therefore an important challenge for the government.

In an attempt to reduce poverty, Nigeria has adopted the UN Millennium Development Goal of reducing by half the proportion of people whose income is less than US$1 a day. They also aim, between 1990 and 2015, to halve the proportion of people who suffer hunger.

Urban environmental problems, such as the scene depicted here on the edge of Kano, are becoming increasingly common.

DEMOCRACY AND THE ECONOMY

First and foremost, the considerable wealth gained from the oil industry needs to be used so that it benefits all Nigerians more equally, and not just a few. The government must create jobs, provide good health and education services and ensure that it is free from corruption. Nigerians need to be able to trust their country's leaders.

For the last 30 years Nigeria has been poorly served by a succession of bad governments. A more stable, democratic and less corrupt government will attract investment from abroad, enabling the country to diversify and exploit more of its valuable resources. This will not only benefit the country in terms of revenues, but will reduce its dependence on oil as its only major resource.

Nigerians would like the international community to recognise that it will be impossible for Nigeria to ever pay back its foreign debts and to write them off.

HIV/AIDS awareness campaigns need to be a top priority for the government if the disease is to be halted.

THE AIDS THREAT

Nigeria is one of five countries in the world identified as being most at risk from the HIV/AIDS virus in the future. In the past, the government has not given it the priority it needs because of political instability and a lack of political will.

There has been a huge increase in the number of HIV/AIDS cases in the last 15 years, though the problem has not been as severe as it has been in southern Africa. However, it would be dangerous for the government to be complacent as the rate of increase in cases is escalating. It is thought that by 2004 about 2.3 million Nigerians had died from AIDS, while 3.8 million were HIV-positive. However, statistics are unreliable because the stigma of AIDS means that people are often reluctant to come forward for treatment.

The government has set up an HIV/AIDS Emergency Action Plan to look at ways in which it can tackle the problem in the short term. However, there are few medical resources available to those who have contracted the virus and most people cannot afford the many drugs that are required to fight it.

BE CAREFUL
AIDS KILLS

Protect The Life Of Every Nigerian By Spreading The MESSAGE Not The VIRUS

COURTESY: NLNG LTD.
BONNY ISLAND.

Many beautiful beaches along the south coast offer great potential for tourism development.

NIGERIA'S REPUTATION ABROAD

Nigeria is notorious for stories of violence, crime, bribery and corruption. Even teachers have been accused of accepting bribes to give students high marks in examinations. Obviously there is truth in this, yet it would be misleading to draw conclusions solely from these claims. The vast majority of Nigerians are honest and hard-working people, and things are already improving since the ending of military rule.

Improving Nigeria's reputation is important to attract not only foreign investment in industries and resources, but also overseas tourists. With its beautiful landscapes and rich heritage, Nigeria has the potential to be a vibrant and fascinating tourist destination, bringing in much-needed foreign currency. Nigeria is of particular interest to the descendants of Black Africans (known as the African Diaspora) who live abroad – mainly in the USA – and who are interested in their personal history and heritage. However, many potential tourists continue to be concerned about the dangers of travelling to Nigeria. A costly infrastructure for tourists, such as safe and efficient transport and accommodation, would need to be developed. However, many Nigerians might suggest that their own basic needs should come first.

ONE NATION?

Nigeria is a country of 137 million people, 500 languages and 36 states – but it is a single nation. Frequent outbreaks of violence between different ethnic and religious groups have led some people to question whether this nation can ever be harmonious. The federation of 36 states was set up in an attempt to address the diversity of Nigeria's population and to allow different areas to have a degree of self-government. But many people feel this is unworkable as it has led to a huge bureaucracy of governors, deputy governors, permanent secretaries, advisers and more. In some cases, 90 per cent of the state's income goes to pay the wages of these people. A proposal that the 36 states be collapsed into six larger and more powerful states is being considered.

Another proposal is that Nigeria is split into

at least two completely separate countries –
an Islamic and Hausa/Fulani north and a
basically Christian and Yoruba/Igbo south. This
would, of course, be problematic because all
the oil wealth would remain in the south.
There are also those who believe passionately
that Nigeria should remain as one nation.

THE FUTURE

Nigeria's greatest asset continues to be its
people. They are energetic and resourceful and
face the problems of everyday life with stoicism
and humour. Nevertheless, some are prepared
to stand up against the corruption they see
around them and there are many strikes and
demonstrations against what they consider
to be injustices. Several Nigerians have been
imprisoned in the past for their stand against
the abuse of human rights in Nigeria.

When Nigerians look to the future they face
many challenges. After years of military rule,
they hope for a more peaceful and stable
future and for the opportunity to benefit from
their country's wealth. Nigeria continues to
have the potential to become a powerful,
industrialised nation – with the right
leadership. Democracy should bring the public

One of the many new government buildings in
Abuja, Nigeria's rapidly expanding capital.

freedom of speech and access to information,
and hopefully will enable people to stamp out
corruption and growing inequality.

With continuing conflict in the Middle East,
Western countries are likely to become more
interested in Nigerian oil to reduce their
dependency on current suppliers such as Iraq
and Saudi Arabia. This could strengthen
Nigeria's position on the world stage.

Nigeria's youth will soon have the country in
their own hands. They are hopeful for a
brighter future.

Air mass A large body of air with common characteristics.

Animism The belief that all living objects have souls.

Arid A term used to describe an environment with an annual rainfall that is below 250–300mm.

Artesian well A well that is drilled through impermeable rock into water-saturated rock. Pressure forces the water to flow upwards.

Biodiversity The variation (diversity) of biological life within an area.

Capital investment Money needed to start up or develop businesses and industry.

Catchment area The geographical area from which streams and tributaries drain into a river, lake or sea.

Census A count of the population.

Colonial A term used to describe a system whereby one country is occupied and ruled by another foreign country.

Commodity An item that can be bought and sold.

Conjunctivitis An infection that causes inflammation of the eye.

Cowpeas A type of legume, also known as field peas.

Crater lake A lake that forms in a bowl-like depression formed by a volcano.

Crude oil Oil in the form in which it is extracted, before it has been refined.

Delta A low area where a river divides before entering a larger body of water, usually a sea or an ocean.

Diversification When a greater variety of industries and businesses are introduced into a country's economy.

Dredging The removal of material from the bottom of a river or estuary.

Drought A prolonged shortage of rainfall.

Ecosystem A system that represents the relationships within a community of living things (plants and animals) and between this community and their non-living surroundings. An ecosystem can be as small as a pond or as large as the Earth.

Equatorial The conditions that exist in the area around the Equator. In climatic terms this usually means hot and wet.

Erosion The way in which the Earth's surface is worn away by the action of water and wind.

Escarpment A steep slope.

Ethnic group People of the same race or nationality who share a distinctive cultural identity.

Federation A country that is divided into regions (states) whose individual governments take greater control of their own affairs with a lesser role for the central government.

GDP (Gross Domestic Product) The monetary value of goods and services produced by a country in a single year.

Glut A situation in which there is so much of a particular product that the price falls.

GNI (Gross National Income) The monetary value of goods and services produced by a country plus any earnings from overseas in a single year. It used to be called Gross National Product (GNP).

Habitat The environment in which any living organism lives.

HEP (hydroelectric power) Electricity generated by water as it passes through turbines.

HIV/AIDS HIV (Human Immunodeficiency Virus) infection leads to AIDS (Acquired Immune Deficiency Syndrome), an illness in which the body's protective system breaks down.

Humidity Wetness in the atmosphere.

Infant mortality rate The number of deaths of infants (0 to 5 years old) per thousand live births.

Infrastructure The basic foundation of a country that includes the roads and railways, bridges, buildings, communication networks and waste disposal systems.

Interest rates The percentage of a borrowed sum of money that is added to it when it is paid back.

Irrigation The controlled addition of water to dry agricultural land in order to improve plant growth.

Islam The religion of Muslims. Muslims believe that there is one God and that Mohammed was the last prophet.

Leaching When water penetrates soil and washes nutrients out of it.

Malnutrition A state when someone has not received enough food or food with enough nutrients.

Mangroves A tropical tree or bush that grows on the edge of salt water. It has prop roots that form a barrier to erosion.

Military coup A sudden and decisive takeover of government by the army, illegally and/or by force.

Missionaries People who try to convert others to their own religion.

Muslim A believer or follower of Islam.

Plantation An area of land where cash crops are grown on a large scale.

Plateau An area of comparatively high, flat land.

Rainforest Dense tropical forest with high rainfall.

Ramadan The ninth month of the Muslim calendar when followers fast during the day.

Reservoirs A lake used to store water. Some reservoirs are artificial.

Rickets A childhood disease caused by a lack of Vitamin D.

Rock strata Different layers of rock.

Sabotage A deliberate act of destruction or disruption in which equipment and machinery is damaged.

Savannah A flat grassland area in tropical or sub-tropical areas.

Sedimentary rocks Rocks that are formed from the accumulation of organic or physical matter.

Self-sufficient Not having to depend on other countries for, for example, food.

Silt Mud, clay or small rocks deposited by a river.

Subsistence farming Farming that provides for the basic needs of the farmer and his family, often with little left over to sell.

Sustainable Something that is capable of lasting and carrying on in the long term.

Terrain A piece of ground with common characteristics.

Thermal spring A natural spring of hot water.

Tributary A stream or river that flows into a larger river.

Undulating Describes a landscape with gently rolling hills.

Urbanisation The process of people moving from the countryside to towns and cities.

Volcanic plugs The resistant rock at the centre of a volcano that remains when the rest of the volcano has been eroded.

Watershed A line that divides two adjacent river basins.

Yam A sweet potato, the root of the plant. It can be baked or boiled and mashed.

FURTHER INFORMATION

BOOKS TO READ:

NON FICTION:

The Changing Face of: Nigeria by Rob Bowden and Roy Maconachie (Hodder Children's Books, 2003) Illustrated reference for KS2–3.

This House Has Fallen by Karl Maier (Penguin Books, 2000) A series of stories recounting the author's experiences of living and working in Nigeria.

A Month and a Day: A Detention Diary by Ken Saro-Wiwa (Penguin, 1995) An account by the writer and environmentalist of his detention by the Nigerian government.

Nations of the World: Nigeria by Bridget Giles (Raintree, 2004) Illustrated reference for in-depth study, with links to KS3–4.

FICTION:

Ake: The Years of Childhood by Wole Soyinka (Africa Book Centre, 1981)

The Famished Road by Ben Okri (Vintage, 1992)

A Forest of Flowers by Ken Saro-Wiwa (Longman African Writers, 1997)

Poems of Black Africa by Wole Soyinka (Hill & Wang, 1975)

Purple Hibiscus by Chimamanda Ngozi Adichie (Fourth Estate, 2004)

Things Fall Apart by Chinua Achebe (Heinemann, 1983)

WEBSITES:

The CIA World Factbook
www.cia.gov/cia/publications/factbook/geos/ni.html
The US Central Intelligence Agency's online factbook, with statistics and assessments of all countries of the world.

All Africa.com
www.allafrica.com/nigeria
Articles and news about Nigeria.

Lonely Planet
www.lonelyplanet.com/destinations/africa/nigeria
General information about Nigeria aimed at travellers.

WWF-UK
www.wwf.org.uk
Search under 'Nigeria' for up-to-date information on environmental issues.

Numbers shown in **bold** refer to pages with maps, graphic illustrations or photographs.

Abuja 9, 13, 45, 53, **57**
  climate **15**
  religion **46**
Achebe, Chinua 48, 54
agriculture *(see also crops, farming)* 10, 18, **23**, **40**, 42
  desertification 33
  economy **25**, **26**
  irrigation 21
  landscape 12, 13

Benin City **9**, 40, 49
Benue, River 10, 11, 12, 13, 16, 17
Biafra 9
British rule 9, 24, 30, 45

civil war 9
climate *(see also rainfall, temperature)* 12, 13, **14**, 15, 32
communication 47, 48, **51**
conservation 36, **37**
corruption 27, 28, 55, 56, 57
crops *(see also agriculture, farming)* **22**, 41, 48, 52
  desertification 33
  exports 23
  imports 26

debt 21, 25, 29, 31, 55
democracy 9, 36, 55, 57
desertification 33, **36**
drought 14, 21, 33, 47

economy *(see also exports, imports, trade)* 24, 27, 28, 30
  urbanisation 40, 41
education *(see also schools)* 25, 31, 39, 40, 47
  emigration 41
  provision 55
  women 53
electricity 16, 30, 42, 43
emigration 41
environmental damage 17, **19**, 36
ethnic groups 8, 16, 45, 46, 47
  disputes 9, 28, 39, 56
Europeans 8, 13, 24
exports *(see also economy)* **25**
  British rule 24
  cocoa 22, 23
  crops 23
  Lagos 45
  oil 19, **20**
  shrimp 23

farming *(see also agriculture, crops)* **16**, 22
  cities 44, 45
  desertification 33
  family 38–39
  habitat threats 34
  migration 41
  pollution 35
  population 39, 42, 43
  traditional methods 36
  women 52
fish **10**, 34, 35
fishing **11**, 23, 35, 48, 52
flooding 15, 17, 34
forests *(see also rainforests, timber)* 10, 36, **37**
Fulani people 8, **42**, 46, 57

gas **20**, 35
GDP (gross domestic product) *(see also economy)* **9**, 29, 58
GNI (gross national income) *(see also economy)* **25**, 58

Hausa people 8, 14, 41, **42**, 46, 47, 48, 57
healthcare 25, **31**, 55
HEP (hydroelectric power) 16, 17, **19**, 58
HIV/AIDS 31, 38, **55**, 58
human rights abuses 9, 29, 57

Ibadan **9**, **15**, **47**, 49
  transport 30
  urbanisation 40
Igbo people 8, 9, 46, 49, 57
imports *(see also economy)* 19, **25**, 26
independence 8, 9, 26
industry **25**, 27, 56
  habitat threats 34
  manufacturing 26, **27**, 44
  mining 13, 21
  oil 18, 19, 21, 31
  steel 27
irrigation 13, **21**, **22**, 36, 58
  desertification 33
  habitat threats 34
  rivers 16, 17

Kano **9**, **44**, **61**
  climate **15**
  desertification 33
  population 39
  urban problems 40, **54**

Lagos 8, 9, 11, **44**, **45**, **46**
  art 48–49
  climate **15**
  industry **24**
  music 49
  pollution **35**
  population 39
  transport 30
  urbanisation 40
Lake Chad 13, 23
languages 8, **9**, 47, 48, 56
leisure 50

mangrove swamps **10**, 11, 32, 34, 58
markets **50**
migration 40, 41, 42, 45
minerals 11, 18, **20**, 21
mining 13, 17, **20**, 21

African dress is often very colourful and is an important part of Nigerian culture.

missionaries 9, 47
mountains 10, 12, 32, 34
music 49

national parks **12**, **37**
Niger Delta 11
  flooding 17
  gas 20
  languages 47
  oil 18, **29**
  pollution 23, 29, **34**, 35
Niger, River 9, 10, 11, 13, **16**, **17**
Nok people 8

oil 8, 9, 11, **18**, **19**
  agriculture 26
  corruption 28
  economy 24, 25
  exports **20**
  pollution 17, **19**, 29, **34**, **35**
  profits 28, 29
  sabotage 31
  urbanisation 40
  wealth 55, 57
oral tradition 47

pollution 8, 35
  Lagos **35**, **45**
  oil 17, **19**, 23, 34, 35
population,
  distribution 39
  ethnic groups 39
  growth 32, 34, 38
  Jos Plateau **13**

rainforests 33
religion 46
rural areas 42, 43
structure **39**
urbanisation 40, **41**
workforce 18
youth **9**
poverty 28, 29, 32, 33, 40, 54

railways *(see also transport)* 30
rainfall *(see also climate)* 13, 14,
  15, 17, **33**
rainforests *(see also forests)* 10, **11**,
  13, **32**, 33, 34, 58
rainy season 14, 41
religion 8, 9, 46, 47
  Abuja 45, **46**
  rivers 16
  violence 56
  women 53
roads *(see also transport)* 30
  development 25
  migration 41
  rainforest **32**, 33

Saro-Wiwa, Ken 29, 35
savannah 12, 13, 32, 34
schools *(see also education)* **47**, 53
shanty towns **40**
slave trade 8, **24**, 45
Sokoto **9**, 33, 40
Soyinka, Wole 48
sport 50, **51**

temperature *(see also climate)* 13,
  14, **15**
timber **32**, 33, 36
tourism 27, **56**
trade *(see also economy)* 8, 24, 43,
  44, 45, 52
transport *(see also railways, roads)*
  16, **17**, **30**, 56

unemployment 28, 31, 40, **45**
urbanisation 40, **41**, 44, **45**, **54**,
  58

water 16, 39, 42, 43, 52
  irrigation 21, 36
  supply 13, 30, 34
wildlife **12**, 37
women **52**, **53**

Yoruba people 46, 48, 49, 51
  cities 44, 45
  empires 8
  states 57
  village **43**

A traffic interchange in Kano, the largest city in northern Nigeria.